THE TEIIDAES...

ERIK D. STOOPS

Faulkner's Publishing Group

This book is dedicated to David Pfeiffer for getting these wonderful books to the hands of many children throughout the world.

Library of Congress Catalog Card Number 97-60522.

COVER PHOTO: Red Tegu Lizard by Terry Odegaard
DESIGNED BY: Graphic Arts & Production, Inc., Plover, WI

Faulkner's Publishing Group
200 Paw Paw Ave. #124
Benton Harbor, MI 49022

©1997 by Erik Daniel Stoops
Faulkner's ISBN 1-890475-05-X Lib

Table of Contents

Chapter One

What are Whiptails, Tegu and Teiidaes?

What is a Whiptail?

Where is the best place to find a Teiidae?

Read on to find these answers and more.

5

by Pat Turcott

▲
THIS IS A BLACK-WHITE TEGU WITH ITS COUSIN, A BABY NILE MONITOR.

What is a Whiptail?

A Whiptail is a reptile. These reptiles have four legs for climbing and swimming. They usually have eyelids, ears and a large powerful tail. Some lizards do not have any legs. *Scientists* have found that certain lizard species are related to their cousin, the snake. The Tegu resembles a snake. The difference between a Tegu and a snake is that the lizard has ears and eyelids while snakes do not.

What is a Teiidae?

Teiidaes are slender reptiles with a thin whip-like tail. They have a divided tongue which they use in their search for food. Most of the 230 species live on the ground and feed on small animals and insects. There are a few species of *unisexual* Teiidaes which lay eggs without being fertilized by a male Teiidae.

A COUSIN OF THE TEGU IS A DUMERILS MONITOR
▼

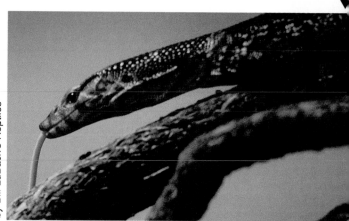

by Bill LuBack's Reptiles

Where do lizards live?

Lizards are located all over the world. The greatest number of species are found in the warm zones: deserts, jungles and rain forests. The only place you cannot find a lizard is in the ice-covered polar regions and where temperatures remain ice-cold year-round.

Photos by Terry Odegaard

▲ THE THICK RAIN FOREST OF COSTA RICA IS HOME TO MANY SPECIES OF WHIPTAILS AND TEGU. THE AUSTRALIAN DESERT IS HOME TO THE BURTON'S LEGLESS LIZARD.

by Terry Odegaard

▲ MANY SPECIES OF LIZARDS MAKE THEIR HOMES IN LARGE TREES LIKE THIS ONE.

Where is the best place to find a lizard?

If I were a lizard, this is where I would be:

- Under a rock
- On a rock
- In a field
- On a house
- In a tree
- In a rain forest

Are Whiptails and Tegu cold-blooded or warm-blooded?

All species of lizards are *cold-blooded*. They need the warm sun during the day to help them move and digest their food.

7

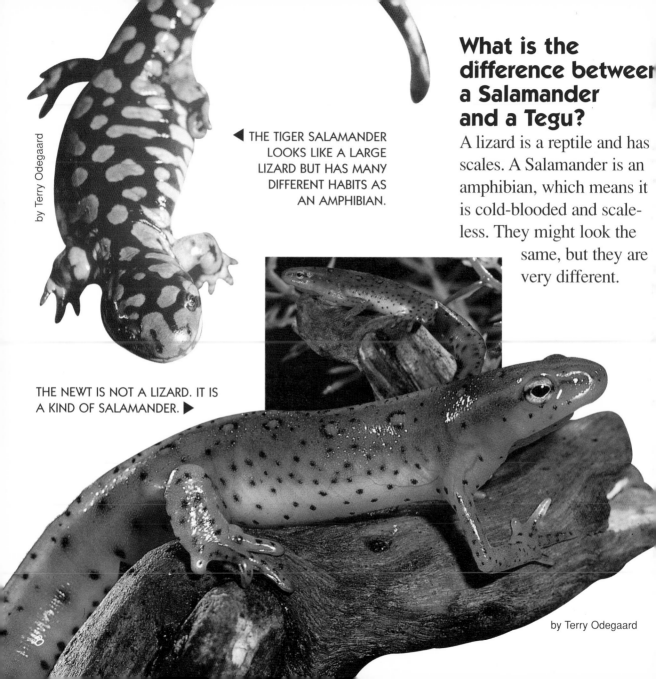

by Terry Odegaard

◀ THE TIGER SALAMANDER
LOOKS LIKE A LARGE
LIZARD BUT HAS MANY
DIFFERENT HABITS AS
AN AMPHIBIAN.

What is the difference between a Salamander and a Tegu?

A lizard is a reptile and has scales. A Salamander is an amphibian, which means it is cold-blooded and scale-less. They might look the same, but they are very different.

THE NEWT IS NOT A LIZARD. IT IS
A KIND OF SALAMANDER. ▶

by Terry Odegaard

GLASS LIZARDS, WORM LIZARDS

Common Glass Lizard:

Scientists call them Glass Lizards because they have the ability to break off their tail to escape from enemies. They live in grass meadows and the pine flatwoods of North Carolina and south Florida. They range from 18 to 42 inches in length and feed on small insects. They are often mistaken for snakes because they have no legs. Unlike snakes, they have movable eyelids and external ear openings.

by Terry Odegaard

▲
GLASS OR LEGLESS LIZARD

Worm Lizard:

This weird, snakelike lizard is found all over the world. They are small, only 7 to 11 inches long, and look like a common earthworm. They have rings of scales encircling their body and tail, and do not have any external ear openings. Some lack external eyes and look blind. They feed on worms, spiders, and termites.

9

Chapter Two

The Lizard's Body

Lizards come in many different shapes and sizes. Their heads are round and some have powerful legs, while some do not have legs at all. Some have large tails, others have spiny tails.

Why does a lizard have scales?

Why does a lizard shed its skin?

This chapter will answer all the questions you may have about a lizard's body.

Why does a lizard have scales?

Many kinds of lizards have different types of scales. Tegu have smooth scales which are used to keep the lizards on their toes while moving across the ground. Some types of Tegu, such as the Dragon Lizard, have rough scales which are used for protection against their enemies.

by Bill LuBack's Reptiles

BLACK-WHITE TEGU.

Why does a lizard shed its skin?

All species of lizards shed their skin. When a lizard sheds its skin, that means it is growing. Some species of lizards such as the Tegu shed in pieces, while other species like the Glass Lizard shed in one whole piece.

How does a lizard shed its skin?

When a lizard sheds its skin, it will find something to rub on such as a rock or a tree branch. It will try to wiggle out of its skin which usually takes a few hours. After the lizard sheds, it will have bright new shiny skin.

Can a Tegu lose its tail?

Yes. Some species of lizards can break their tail off when an enemy grabs it or if they are frightened. The tail often grows back in a few months.

What is the large scale on the bottom near the tail?

The large scale located between the back legs near the tail is called an ***anal plate***. This is where the lizard discharges its wastes and also where the reproductive organs are located.

How do lizards' muscles work?

Some species of lizard, such as the Red Tegu, have strong muscles that enable them to dig, lift rocks and climb trees.

How do lizards' bones work?

Lizards' bones work a lot like our bones. They have knees, fingers, ribs and a spinal column. They are often flexible which help lizards move around.

Are lizards' legs powerful, and what are they used for?

Some species of lizards such as the Whiptail Lizard from Arizona have very powerful legs to help them catch food and run away from their enemies.

◀ DUMERILS MONITOR

by Bill LuBack's Reptiles

IF YOU LOOK VERY CLOSELY YOU CAN SEE THE FRONT LEGS OF THIS TEGU. THEY ARE VERY POWERFUL AND ARE USED FOR DIGGING AND RUNNING.

What do lizards die from?

Many lizards die from diseases caused by *viruses* and bacteria which they can catch from other lizards. Lizards can catch colds, cough and sneeze like we do. They also die from stress due to being held in captivity. They can die from *parasites* that crawl on their body and from parasites that reside in their body. *Poachers* may often kill lizards for their skin or catch them to sell to people. This is not very fair to the lizards.

Can lizards swim?

Some species of lizards, like the Water Dragon, are great swimmers. They use their legs and tail to help them glide in the water.

Can lizards climb trees?

Yes. The Tree Lizards of southwestern United States desert spend much of their lives in trees and are wonderful climbers.

13

Chapter Three

Senses

Lizards have some of the strangest senses of all reptiles. What would it be like to smell with your tongue and have eyelids without eyelashes?

Do lizards have ears?

Do they have eyelids?

These are some of the questions you will find in this chapter.

Do lizards sleep?

Yes. Some species of lizards, such as the Glass Lizard, sleep at night. Others, like the Dragon Lizard, sleep during the day and are active all night long.

Do lizards have eyelids?

Yes. Unlike snakes, all species of lizards have eyelids. Like our eyelids, they protect the lizard's eyes from dirt and predators.

by Bill LuBack's Reptiles

BLACK-WHITE TEGU

by Bill LuBack's Reptiles

BLACK-WHITE TEGU

Do lizards have ears?

Yes. Lizards' ears are two tiny holes located near the eyes. They can hear vibrations in the air to help them find food and stay safe from their enemies.

Can lizards see colors?

Scientists have found that certain species of lizards can see colors such as reds and yellows. Many scientists are still learning about these spectacular findings.

15

Chapter Four

Eating Habits

Lizards eat both plants and animals
depending on the species.

However, they like to eat a variety of
different plants and animals.

In this chapter you will find out what they like to eat and
how different prey help them live every day.

Do lizards eat other lizards?

Yes. Some species of lizard, such as the Black-White Tegu, feed on smaller lizards. The Dragon Lizard of Brazil has been known to eat its own kind.

Do lizards throw up?

When lizards become sick or eat something that doesn't agree with them, they often throw up. This is sometimes harmful to lizards because they tend to become dehydrated when this happens.

by Bill LuBack's Reptiles

Do lizards chew their food?

No. Lizards swallow their food whole. They use their teeth for tearing chunks and then swallow. Some lizards have very small teeth and may use their tongue to help them eat.

THE DUMERILS MONITOR IS A
COUSIN OF THE TEGU.

Chapter Five

Lizard Reproduction

Do lizards make good parents?

How many babies do lizards have?

Read on to answer these answers and more.

Do lizards give live birth?

They give birth the same way as an egg-laying species, through the anal plate. The **neonates**, "new-borns" will often be born in an egg yolk placenta sack, which they usually break out of at birth. Baby lizards use their egg tooth to do this. The egg tooth usually falls off in about a week. Sometimes the mother lizard will eat the placenta sacks. This provides nutrition for the exhausted mother lizards.

Do lizards make good parents?

No. Most species do not make good parents. After the mother lays her eggs, she may never see the offspring again.

by Bill LuBack's Reptiles

▲

A BABY TEGU HAS JUST HATCHED.

How many babies do lizards have?

Depending on the species, lizards will have from two to thirty babies at one time. A large Water Monitor may lay up to 30 eggs. The Shingleback Skink may have two to three live babies.

How do lizards mate?

According to scientists, most of the Whiptail Lizard species of the southwestern United States are **unisexual**, meaning males are absent. A special hormone in the female helps the mother lizard produce eggs which only grow into females. Lizards mate, depending on the species, during the spring or rainy season of their geographic location.

Chapter Six

Lizards and People

If we see a lizard in the wild, what should we do?

Why are some lizards hunted and killed?

Read on to discover these answers and more.

by Wai Lui

ENDANGERED

What does endangered species mean?

The word *endangered* means a species threatened with extinction. Every day a number of species of animals becomes endangered or even extinct.

by Terry Odegaard

THE RED TEGU IS VERY POPULAR WITH COLLECTORS. WE SHOULD HAVE LAWS TO PROTECT THEM IN THE WILD STATE.

Why are some lizards so very rare?

Many species such as the Black Legless Lizard are very rare because of habitat destruction. Other species of lizards are losing their homes because the rain forests are being cut down. We should protect all species of lizards and animals in all areas.

Why are some lizards hunted and killed?

Some species of lizards are very popular on the pet trade and are often captured for this reason. Some species are killed for no reason at all.

If I want to see a lizard, where should I look?

The safest place to see a lizard is at a zoo. Many zoos have several kinds of species on display from all over the world. It is best not to catch lizards from the wild and keep them in your home. Try to leave them where they belong.

by Terry Odegaard

◄ HABITATS SUCH AS THIS OPEN FIELD ARE OFTEN BULL-DOZED AND DEVELOPED FOR HOUSES. THIS CAN MAKE LIZARDS VERY RARE.

DUMERILS MONITORS ARE COUSINS OF THE TEGU.
▼

If we see a lizard in the wild, what should we do?

The best thing to do is to leave it alone. Many kinds of lizards like to eat bugs around your house. This is a very good thing and you should enjoy the wonderful opportunity to view these creatures.

by Bill LuBack's Reptiles

23

If I want to be a scientist and study lizards, what will I be?

If you want to study lizards when you grow up, you can become a *herpetologist*. Many herpetologists spend their whole lives trying to protect and conserve different species of lizards.

What can I do to protect lizards?

The best thing to do to protect lizards is to pick up litter and throw it in a garbage receptacle, and leave the lizards alone. You should learn more about the lizards in your area so you can help protect them. It is very rewarding when you do this and makes you feel good.

DUMERILS ▶
MONITOR

by Bill Luback's Reptiles

BLACK-WHITE TEGU WITH COUSIN BABY MONITOR

Do Tegu have any cousins?

Yes. The Monitor Lizard is a cousin of the Tegu. The main difference between these two is the Monitor is more primitive.

What is the rarest Tegu?

The Water Tegu of South America is a very hard-to-find lizard. There are very few of these species in zoos.

Chapter Seven

Lizard Facts

Are lizards related to dinosaurs?

What is the smallest species of Whiptail Lizards?

Read on to find many interesting facts about lizards.

Let's classify Snake Lizards:

The *family* of Snake Lizard is Pygopodidae.

31 Species in 8 Genera. (Several closely related species make up one Genus.)

Let's classify Whiptails and Racerunners:

The *family* of Whiptail and Racerunner is Teiidae.

227 Species in 39 Genera. Some interesting species include: Caiman Lizard, Black-White Tegu, Red Tegu, Western Racerunner.

by Terry Odegaard

BLACK-WHITE TEGU LIZARD

Are lizards related to dinosaurs?

According to herpetologists and scientists, many species of reptiles, including lizards, were thought to be related to the dinosaurs. This is still up for debate. *Paleontologists* have found that the dinosaurs were more closely related to birds. According to scientists, some species of Glass Lizards were discovered around 30 million years ago.

by Terry Odegaard

◀ RED TEGU LIZARD 27

What is the largest Whiptail species?

The Caiman Lizard which resembles a small type of crocodile called a Caiman reaches a length of three feet.

What is the smallest species of Whiptail Lizards?

The Little Striped Whiptail Lizard reaches a length of about six inches.

Where are Whiptail Lizards found?

They are found in southwestern United States, throughout South America and in the West Indies, except for Patagonia.

by Pat Turcott

BAJA BLUE ROCK LIZARD

Where did the Whiptail get its name?

Its name comes from its large, whip-like tail. This can be seen on species from the southwestern part of the United States.

Where are Glass Lizards found?

Some species like the Eastern Glass Lizard, are found in southeastern United States. Other species are found in Aru, New Britain, New Guinea and Australia.

What makes Glass Lizards different from other lizard species?

Good question! Their body is snakelike in appearance and their forelimbs are absent. It's named the Glass Lizard because of its very fragile tail.

◀ GLASS LIZARD

by Terry Odegaard

Lizards that are currently threatened or in danger of becoming extinct:

ENDANGERED

Rodrigues Day Gecko
Indian Ocean

St. Croix Ground Lizard
Virgin Islands

Culebra Giant Anole
Puerto Rico

Black Legless Lizard
USA

Fiji Banded Iguana
Fiji, Tonga

Anegada Ground Iguana
Virgin Islands

San Joaquin Leopard Lizard
USA

Hierro Giant Lizard
Canary Islands

▲
BLACK-WHITE TEGU

by Terry Odegaard

Glossary

Anal Plate:
The large scale between the back legs of the lizard.

Chlamydosaurus King II:
A scientific name for frilled lizard.

Cold-Blooded:
Having a body temperature not internally regulated, but approximately that of the environment.

Endangered: Threatened with extinction.

Endemic:
Native to a particular country, nation or region.

External:
Having merely the outward appearance of something.

Fossil:
A remnant impression, or trace of an animal or plant of past geological ages that has been preserved in the earth's crust.

Herpetologist:
One who studies reptiles and amphibians.

Neonate: Newborn.

Paleontologist:
One who studies the science dealing with the life of past geological periods as known from fossil remains.

Parasite:
An organism that lives in or on another organism at whose expense it receives nourishment.

Poacher:
One who kills or takes game and fish illegally.

Quadrupole:
A system composed of two dipoles of equal but oppositely directed moment.

Rhynchocephalian:
A class of reptile.

Scientist:
A scientific investigator.

Unisexual:
All individuals are females that can lay eggs and are fertile without mating.

Virus:
The causative agent of an infectious disease.

Warm-Blooded:
Having a relatively high and constant body temperature relatively independent of the surroundings.

Books and CD-Roms Written by the Author Suggested Reading

Snakes and Other Reptiles of the Southwest

Erik D. Stoops & Annette T. Wright. 1991. Golden West Publishing Company, Phoenix, Arizona. Scientific Field Guide.

Snakes

Erik D. Stoops & Annette T. Wright. 1992. Hardback and Paperback. Sterling Publishing Company, New York. Children's non-fiction, full-color, question and answer format. First Book in Children's Nature Library Series.

Breeding Boas and Pythons

Erik D. Stoops & Annette T. Wright. 1993. TFH Publishing Company, New York. Scientific Care and Breeding Guide.

Sharks

Erik D. Stoops & Sherrie L. Stoops. Illustrated by Jeffrey L. Martin. June, 1994. Hardback and Paperback. Sterling Publishing Company, New York. Children's non-fiction, full-color, question and answer format. Second Book in Children's Nature Library Series.

Dolphins

Erik D. Stoops, Jeffrey L. Martin & Debbie L. Stone. Release date, January, 1995. Hardback and Paperback. Sterling Publishing Company, New York. Children's non-fiction, full-color, question and answer format. Third Book in Children's Nature Library Series.

Whales

Erik D. Stoops, Jeffrey L. Martin & Debbie L. Stone. Release date, March, 1995. Hardback and Paperback. Sterling Publishing Company, New York. Children's non-fiction, full-color, question and answer format. Fourth Book in Children's Nature Library Series.

Scorpions and Other Venomous Insects of the Desert

Erik D. Stoops & Jeffrey L. Martin. Release date, June, 1995. Golden West Publishing Company, Phoenix, Arizona. A user-friendly guide.

Alligators and Crocodiles

Erik D. Stoops & Debbie L. Stone. Release date, October, 1994. Sterling Publishing Company, New York. Children's non-fiction, full-color, question and answer format. Fifth Book in Children's Nature Library Series.

Wolves

Erik D. Stoops & Dagmar Fertl. Release date, December, 1996. Sterling Publishing Company, New York. Children's non-fiction, full-color, question and answer format. Sixth Book in Children's Nature Library Series.

Internet Sites:

Zoo Net:
http://www.mindspring.com/~zoonet

Herp Link:
http://home.ptd.net/~herplink/index.html

Erik Stoops:
http://www.primenet.com/~dink

Look for the Adventures of Dink the Skink Children's book series and animated CD Rom Stories coming out in 1997.

INDEX

WE WOULD LIKE TO THANK THE FOLLOWING PEOPLE FOR THEIR ENCOURAGEMENT AND PARTICIPATION:
NATIONAL ZOOLOGICAL PARK, OFFICE OF PUBLIC AFFAIRS, SUSAN BIGGS, SMITHSONIAN INSTITUTION, TERRY CHRISTOPHER, TERRY ODEGAARD, CINCINNATI ZOO AND BOTANICAL GARDENS, ST. LOUIS ZOO, BILL LUBACK'S REPTILES, INC., AMANDA JAKSHA, JESSIE COHEN, PAT TURCOTT, RODNEY FREEMAN, DIANE E. FREEMAN, STEVEN CASTANEDA, CLYDE PEELINGS OF REPTILELAND, MICKEY OLSEN OF WILDLIFE WORLD ZOO, SCOTTSDALE CHILDREN'S NATURE CENTER, DR. JEAN ARNOLD, ARIZONA GAME AND FISH DEPARTMENT, ERIN DEAN OF THE UNITED STATES FISH AND WILDLIFE SERVICE, BOB FAULKNER, DAVE PFEIFFER OF EDUCATION ON WHEELS FOR MAKING THIS PROJECT A REALITY, DR. MARTY FELDMAN, SHERRIE STOOPS, ALESHA STOOPS, VICTORIA AND JESSICA EMERY.